# The Higher Education Of The Soul

**Rudolf Steiner**

# Kessinger Publishing's Rare Reprints

## Thousands of Scarce and Hard-to-Find Books on These and other Subjects!

- Americana
- Ancient Mysteries
- Animals
- Anthropology
- Architecture
- Arts
- Astrology
- Bibliographies
- Biographies & Memoirs
- Body, Mind & Spirit
- Business & Investing
- Children & Young Adult
- Collectibles
- Comparative Religions
- Crafts & Hobbies
- Earth Sciences
- Education
- Ephemera
- Fiction
- Folklore
- Geography
- Health & Diet
- History
- Hobbies & Leisure
- Humor
- Illustrated Books
- Language & Culture
- Law
- Life Sciences

- Literature
- Medicine & Pharmacy
- Metaphysical
- Music
- Mystery & Crime
- Mythology
- Natural History
- Outdoor & Nature
- Philosophy
- Poetry
- Political Science
- Science
- Psychiatry & Psychology
- Reference
- Religion & Spiritualism
- Rhetoric
- Sacred Books
- Science Fiction
- Science & Technology
- Self-Help
- Social Sciences
- Symbolism
- Theatre & Drama
- Theology
- Travel & Explorations
- War & Military
- Women
- Yoga
- *Plus Much More!*

**We kindly invite you to view our catalog list at:
http://www.kessinger.net**

# VII

# THE HIGHER EDUCATION
# OF THE SOUL

IF a man carries out the culture of his thoughts and feelings and emotions in the way already described in the chapters on Probation, Enlightenment, and Initiation, he then effects a change in his soul such as Nature has effected in his body. Before this training, soul and spirit are undifferentiated masses. In such a state the clairvoyant will perceive them as interlacing clouds, rotating spirally, and having usually a dull glimmer of reddish or reddish-brown color, or, perhaps, of reddish-yellow; but after this growth they begin to assume a brilliant yellowish-green or yellow-blue hue, and become of a regular structure. A man attains such regularity of structure, and at the same time the higher knowledge, when he brings into the realm of his thoughts, feelings and emotions, an order, such as Nature has brought into his bodily organs, by means of which he can see, hear, digest, breathe, speak and so forth. Gradually the student learns, as it were, to breathe, to see with the soul, and to speak and hear with the spirit.

In the following pages a few of the practical points pertaining to the higher education of the soul and spirit will be more fully treated. They are such as may be practically attained by anyone without additional instruction, and by means of which a further step in occult science may be taken.

A particular kind of discipline must be patiently attempted such as to avoid every emotion of impatience, for it produces a paralyzing, yea, even a deadening, effect on the higher faculties within us. One must not expect immeasurable glimpses of the higher worlds to open out before one from day to day, for assuredly, as a rule, this does not occur. Contentment with the smallest progress, repose and tranquility must more and more possess the soul. It is conceivable, of course, that the learner may impatiently expect results, but he will attain nothing so long as he fails to master this impatience. Nor is it of any use to struggle against this impatience in the ordinary way, for then it will only become stronger than ever. It is thus that men deceive themselves, for in such a case it embeds itself all the more firmly in the depths of the soul. It is only by repeatedly surrendering oneself to a single definite thought, and by making it absolutely one's own, that anything is really attained. One should think: "I must certainly do everything possible for the culture of soul and spirit, but I will work tranquilly until, by higher powers, I shall be found worthy of definite illumination." When this thought has become so powerful in a man that it is an actual trait in his character, he is treading the right path. This trait will then express itself even in external affairs. The gaze of the eye becomes tranquil; the movements of the body become sure; the resolutions defined; and all that we call nervous susceptibility gradually disappears. Rules that seem trifling and insignificant must be taken into account. For example, suppose that someone affronts us. Before we receive this occult education, we would have directed our resentment against the wrong-doer; there would have been an uprush of anger within us. But in such a case the occult student will think to himeslf: "An affront of this kind can make no difference to my worth," and whatever must be done to meet the affront, he accomplishes with calm and composure, not with passion. To him it is not a matter of how an affront is to be borne, but without hesitation he is led to ignore or punish the affront to his own person in exactly the same way as if it had been offered to another, in which case one has the right to resent or disregard it. It must always be remembered, however, that the occult training is perfected not by coarse external processes, but by subtle, silent alterations in the life of thought and emotion.

Patience has an attractive, while impatience has a repellent, effect on the treasures of the higher knowledge. In the higher regions of being, nothing can be attained by haste and restlessness. Desire and longing for immediate results must be silenced, for these are qualities of the soul before which all higher knowledge recedes. However precious this knowledge may be accounted, one must not desire to anticipate the time of its coming. And, furthermore, he who wishes to have it for his own sake alone will never attain it. It is absolutely demanded that one should be true to himself in his innermost soul. One must not there be deceived by anything; he must encounter, face to face and with absolute truthfulness, his own faults, failings, and unfitness. The moment you try to excuse to yourself any one of your weaknesses, you place an obstacle in the way which leads upward. There is one way only by which to get rid of such obstacles. Our faults and weaknesses can be removed only by self-illumination, and that is by correctly understanding them. All that is needed lies latent in the human soul and can be evoked. A man immediately improves his understanding and his reason when in repose he makes it clear to himself why he is weak in any respect. Self-knowledge of this kind is naturally difficult, for the temptation to deceive oneself is immeasurably great. He who is accustomed to be truthful with himself has opened the portals into a deeper insight.

138

All curiosity must fall away from the student. He must wean himself as much as possible from inquiries into matters of which he wishes to know only for the gratification of his personal thirst for superficial information. He must ask himself only what things will assist him in the perfection of his innermost being for the service of the general evolution. Nevertheless, his delight in knowledge and his devotion to it must in no degree become relaxed. He must listen devoutly to all that contributes to such an end, and should seek every opportunity of doing so.

For this interior culture it is especially necessary that the desire-life should be carefully educated. One must not become wholly destitute of desire, for if we are to accomplish something it is necessary that we should desire it, and a desire will always be fulfilled if a certain special force is behind it. This particular force results from a right knowledge: "Do not desire at all until you know the true conditions of any sphere." That is one of the golden rules for the occult student. The wise man first ascertains the laws of the world, and then his desires become powers which realize themselves. Let us consider an example in which the effect is evident. There are certainly many who would like to learn from their own intuition something about their life before birth. Such a desire is altogether aimless, and leads to no result so long as the person in question has not acquired a knowledge of the laws that govern the nature of the Eternal, and a knowledge of them in their subtlest and most intimate character. But if he has actually acquired this knowledge and then wishes to pass onward, he is able to do so by his elevated and purified desire.

Moreover, it is of no use to say to oneself: "Yes, I will forthwith examine my previous life, and study with that aim in view." One must rather be ready to abandon such desire, to eliminate it altogether, and first of all, learn, without consideration of this aim. One should cultivate devotion to knowledge without regard to desires. It is only then that one enters into possession of the desire which we are considering, in a way that leads to its own fulfilment.

From one's anger or vexation arises an adverse condition in the spiritual world, so that those forces which would open the eyes of the soul are turned away. For example, if someone should annoy me, he sends forth a current into the world of the soul. So long as I allow myself to be annoyed, I cannot see this current. My own annoyance clouds it. But from this it must not be supposed that when I no longer feel annoyed I will see the astral vision. To see an astral vision it is indispensable that the eye of the soul should already be developed; but the capacity for sight of this kind is latent in everyone. And again it is true that during the development, so long as one can be annoyed the sight remains inactive; nor does it present itself immediately, when one has overcome to a small extent this feeling of annoyance. One must continually persevere in the struggle with such a feeling, and patiently make progress: then, some day, he will find that this eye of the soul has become fully developed. Of course annoyance is not the only quality with which we have to struggle before attaining this end. Many people grow impatient or sceptical, because they have for years cultivated certain qualities of the soul and yet clairvoyance has not ensued. They have developed only a few qualities and have allowed others to run wild. The gift of clairvoyance first manifests itself when all those qualities which do not permit the development of the latent faculties are suppressed. Undoubtedly the beginnings of such hearing and seeing may appear at an earlier period, but these are only young and tender shoots which are subject to all possible error, and which, if they be not carefully fostered, may quickly die.

The qualities which have to be combated, in addition to anger and vexation, are such as ambition, timidity, curiosity, superstition, conceit, the disease of prejudice, idle love of gossip, and the making of distinctions in regard to human beings according to the merely outward marks of rank, sex, race, and so forth. In our time it is difficult for people to comprehend that the combating of such qualities can have any connection with an increase of capacity for knowledge. But every devotee of Occultism is aware that much more depends upon such matters than upon the expansion of the intellect or the employment of artificial practices. It is particularly easy for a misunderstanding of this point to arise, inasmuch as many believe that one should cultivate foolhardiness because one must be fearless, and that one should ignore altogether the differences in men because one has to combat the prejudices of race, rank, and so forth. Rather should one first learn to appreciate these differences correctly, then one is no longer entangled in prejudice. Even in the usual sense it is true that a fear of any phenomenon hinders one from estimating it rightly; that a race-prejudice prevents one from looking into a man's soul. The student of Occultism must bring his common-sense to perfection in all its exactitude and subtlety.

Even everything that a man says without having clearly thought it out will place an obstacle in the path of his occult education. At the same time we must here consider one point which can only be elucidated by giving an example. Thus, if anyone should say something to which another must reply, the one replying should be careful to consider the intention, the feelings, even the prejudices of this other person, rather than what he has to say at the moment on the subject under discussion. In other words, the student must apply himself keenly to the cultivation of a certain fine tact. He must learn to judge how much it may mean to this other person if his opinion be opposed. It must not be imagined for a moment that he ought for this reason, to withhold his own opinion. One must give to the questioner as careful a hearing as possible, and from what one has heard, formulate one's own reply. In such cases there is a certain thought which will constantly recur to the student, and he is treading the true path if this thought becomes so vital within him that it grows into a trait of his character. The thought is as follows: "It matters little whether my view be different from his, the vital point is whether he will discover the right view for himself if I am able to contribute something towards it." By thoughts of such a kind, the mode of action and the character of the student will become permeated with gentleness, one of the most essential qualities for the reception of occult teaching. Harshness obscures that internal image which ought to be evoked by the eye of the soul, while by gentleness many obstacles are cleared from the way, and the inner organs opened.

Along with this gentleness another trait will

presently be developed in the soul. He will make a quiet estimate of all the subtleties in the soul-life around him, without considering the emotions of his own soul. And if this condition has been attained, the soul-emotions in the environment of others will have such an effect on him that the soul within him grows, and, growing, becomes organized, as a plant expands in the sunlight. Gentleness, quiet reserve, and true patience, open the soul to the world of souls, and the spirit to the realm of spirits. Persevere in repose and retirement; close the senses to that which they brought you before you began your training; bring into utter stillness all those thoughts which, in accordance with your previous habits, were tossed up and down within you; become quite still and silent within, wait in patience, and then the tranquil higher worlds will begin to develop the sight of your soul and the hearing of your spirit. Do not suppose that you will *immediately* see and hear in the worlds of soul and spirit, for all that you are doing does but help the development of your higher senses, and you will not be able to see with the soul and to hear with the spirit before you have to some degree acquired those senses. When you have persevered for a time in repose and retirement, then go about your daily affairs, having first impressed upon your mind the thought: "Some day, when I am ready, I shall attain what I am to attain."

144

Finally: "Make no attempt whatever to attract any of these higher powers to yourself by an effort of the will." These are instructions which every occult student receives from his teacher at the entrance of the way. If he observes them, he then improves himself; and if he does not observe them, all his labor is in vain; but they are difficult of achievement for him only who has not patience and perseverance. No other obstacles exist save those which one places for oneself, and these may be avoided by anyone if he really wills it. It is necessary to continually insist upon this point, because many people form an altogether wrong conception of the difficulty that lies in the path of Occultism. In a certain sense, it is easier to accomplish the earlier steps of the occult way, than it is for one who has received no instruction, to get rid of the difficulties of one's every-day life. In addition to this, it must be understood that only such things are here imparted as are attended by no danger to the health of soul or body. There are certain other ways which lead more quickly to the goal, but it is not well to treat of them publicly, because they may sometimes have certain effects on a man which would necessitate the immediate intervention of an experienced teacher, and in any case would require his continual supervision. Now, as something about these quicker ways frequently forces itself into publicity, it becomes necessary to give express warning against entering upon them without personal guidance. For reasons which only the initiated can understand, it will never be possible to give public instruction concerning these other ways in their true form, and the fragments which here and there make their appearance can never lead to anything profitable, but may easily result in the undermining of health, fortune and peace of mind. He who does not wish to put himself in the power of certain dark forces, of whose nature and origin he may know nothing, had far better avoid meddling in such matters.

Something may here be added concerning the environment in which the practices of occult instruction ought to be undertaken. This is of great importance, although for almost every man the case is different. He who practices in an environment which is only filled with selfish interests, as for example, the modern struggle for existence, ought to be sure that these interests are without influence upon the development of his spiritual organs. It is true that the inner laws of these organs are so powerful that this influence cannot be fatally injurious. Just as a lily, however inappropriate the environment in which it may be placed, can never become a thistle, so the eye of the soul can never grow to anything but its destined end, even though it be subjected to all the modern reverse influences. But it is well if, under all circumstances, the student should now and then seek for his environment the quietude, the inner dignity, the sweetness of Nature herself. Especially fortunate are the conditions of him who is able to pursue his occult studies in the green world of plants, or among the sunny mountains or the delightful interplay of simple things. This develops the inner organs in a degree of harmony which is difficult to obtain amid the noise and commercialism of a modern city. He also is more favorably situated than the mere townsman, who, during his childhood at least, was able to breathe the perfume of the pines, to gaze on the snowy peaks, or observe the silent activity of woodland creatures and insects. Yet no one who is obliged to live in a city should fail to give his evolving soul and spirit the nurture that comes from the inspired utterances of the mighty teachers of man. He who cannot every springtime follow day by day the unfolding of the greenwood, ought in its place to draw into his heart the sublime doctrines of the *Bhagavad Gîtâ,* or of *St. John's Gospel,* or of Thomas à Kempis. There are various paths to the summit of insight, but a right selection is invaluable.

The adept in Occultism could, indeed, say much concerning these paths—much that might seem strange to an uninitiated hearer. For example, suppose that someone has advanced far along the occult path, and wholly unaware of his nearness, may be standing at the entrance to the sight of the soul and the hearing of the spirit, and then he has the good fortune to pass peacefully into its very presence, and a bandage falls away from the eyes of his soul. Suddenly he can see—his vision is attained! Another, it may be, has advanced so far that this bandage needs only to be loosened, and by some stroke of destiny this occurs. For another one this very stroke might actually have the effect of paralyzing his powers and undermining his energy, but for the occult student it becomes the occasion of his enlightenment. Perhaps a third has patiently persevered for years, and without any marked result. Suddenly, while tranquilly seated in his quiet chamber, light envelops him, the walls become transparent, they vanish away, and a new world expands before his opened eyes, or is audible to his awakened spirit.

This is the end of this publication.

Any remaining blank pages are for our book binding
requirements and are blank on purpose.

To search thousands of interesting publications like this one,
please remember to visit our website at:

http://www.kessinger.net

Printed in the United States
125739LV00001B/6/A

9 781425 455033